Bridleless Riding, Using Positive Reinforcement

Claire Bruff

DISCLAIMER: Horses are flight animals and, despite our best efforts, will always remain somewhat unpredictable. Because of this, the author cannot be held liable for any accident or injury sustained through following the guidelines in this book. This book is for general educational purposes. Any action on the part of the reader based on the information held in this book is made solely at the discretion of the reader.

Acknowledgements:

I would like to thank my wonderful husband for not only giving me the kick up the backside to finally sit down and get what I do in everyday life onto paper and into a book but also for proof reading, getting all of the computer side done and even illustrating it for me! I couldn't have done it without you!

Thank you to my lovely boys, Noah and Elijah who have had to live with a distracted mum for a little while as this non-academic wrestled with pen and paper.

Thank you to Claire Bettinson for having a read beforehand to make sure it all made sense and also to the lovely Becky Charnock for using her skills to spot any mistakes and nonsense.

I'm aware that ponies can't read, but I owe a huge thank you to each and every horse and pony that I've worked with and trained; they have taught me everything you will read about in this book and more.

About me:

As a child I loved everything about horses: how they smelt, how they moved, how they gave me a sense of freedom that I had never felt before. I started riding at my local riding school at the age of eleven, never thought twice about putting a bit into my horse's mouth, about whacking him with the stick in my hand, or about giving him a huge kick with my legs if he didn't do what I wanted him to do. In fact, I was encouraged by my instructor to do exactly that! It was all about *my* enjoyment, *my* fulfilment and *my* personal goals.

When I was blessed enough to meet Bella and call her my own, it was her who made me question the way I was working with her (or not working with her as the case was). Our rides would be difficult, as we would work against each other rather than as one. I'd get emotional and angry, wondering why she wouldn't just submit and do what I was asking of her. Even in our lessons she would be strong. I remember very clearly one particular day after another fight in the arena, where I came away with tears in my eyes and blisters on my fingers from trying so hard to 'get her into an outline'. I took the bridle off, attached the reins to a halter and it was like someone had sprinkled fairy dust over the two of us. We were together, as one, the fighting was non-existent, and we were both happier. I remember feeling deflated that I hadn't listened to what she was trying to tell me and this took me down a very un-used back road, you know, the kind of track that you often find on a forgotten bridleway with many fallen trees, overgrown hedges, where the ground beneath is tricky terrain so you have to trust your horse and where she chooses to place her feet. We went on a long journey where I learnt to tune into her so intently and I finally understood that she wasn't there for me to use; she wasn't a machine that had no thoughts or feelings; she wasn't a robot that I could computerize to perform a sequence of patterns. She had a mind of her own and it was up to me to not only listen but to respect her as the sentient being she really was.

Despite all of this, bridleless riding with her felt out of reach. I'd watch beautiful videos on YouTube of young girls with flowing hair and tackless horses galloping through fields with not a care in the world and I'd long for that but this chestnut mare was very talkative: if she wanted to do something then she would do it. However, I started to use the cordeo more and more but never actually predominantly used it with her until one day whilst she was in season and joggy and I was trying to tell myself to not pull on the reins but instead to ask her to compromise, I remembered that day in the arena where I had an emotional moment and did something in the same vein. I leant forward, pulled the bridle from her face and right there and then she tuned in and she listened in a way that I'd never seen from her before. I felt a freedom, a deepening that we'd never experienced together. Looking back, I wouldn't advise this to any of my clients and there are steps to transition to bridleless safely which is what this book is all about!

I have many people telling me I am so brave riding across Dartmoor without a bridle. They tell me that I must really trust my horse, but I am here to tell you that it really isn't all about trust. It isn't about being this special, gifted, horse whisperer person. There is no magic spell that you must recite three times and with a click of your little heels, voila your horse is now bridleless and off you go. I am just a normal person who loses welly boots in the mud and who sometimes ends up arse over tit in the quagmire that is British weather. I get caught up in lead ropes just like you. Flipping heck I even lost my footing as I was dismounting one day and had to be air lifted to hospital as a result! I've been barged and the horse has run off into the night, I've been kicked, I've been bitten. I am just a normal person who has good days and bad days (mostly good since using positive reinforcement training) with my horses so if I can train to ride bridleless then I'm telling you, YOU can 100% do it too! You just have to be committed to learning, growing and never standing still in your thirst for knowledge and being here tells me that is what you are doing. It is simply about the training and the time that you put into it. Just like a horse that is trained to be ridden with a bit, to move forward when pressure is applied continuously with the leg, to pick up the pace when a whip is applied, bridleless riding is about training.

I went on to train as an equine behaviourist and trainer and an Emmett muscle release therapist not only because I love every second I spend around horses but because it is my way of giving something back to them when they have given me so much.

CONTENTS:

About This Book:

A lot of people tell me that they can't go bitless let alone bridleless with their horse because it's 'crazy' or 'too highly strung' or 'has too much of a mind of its own'. The truth is I believe every horse can go bridleless but not every rider can. There are a few things that need to be harmonious for it to work including:

- training,
- confidence in the training and
- understanding that control isn't part of that training.

I have one of those 'highly strung horses' with 'a mind of its own' and we ride the moor bridleless and she listens and (so far) we've never ended up bolting off into the sunset. Riding bridleless can be achieved and I have successfully ridden this way with numerous different horses. The steps in this book, along with listening to the horse in front of you, work effectively and here's the best news: anyone can put them into practice!

Whilst I will give you the tools to get to a place where you can ride bridleless, it's up to you to put the time into the training and realise every single horse is different. So, take these tools and use them but be intuitive, listen to the horse in front of you and respond according to their needs and thresholds in every given moment.

Who's it for?

This book is for anyone who would like to take the path down yonder to bridleless riding whilst delving lightly into positive reinforcement training along the way. It's for the person who wants the practical without the academic, who wants a short read without the heaviness that some books might bring. It's for young and old so come one, come all.

What You Will and Won't Find in this Book:

Before you delve into the pages of this book I thought it might be helpful to quickly touch on what you will and won't find within its pages. I know we all have expectations and if you're anything like me then you like to know what's ahead: no surprises!

What you WILL find is:

- A STEP BY STEP GUIDE ON HOW TO RIDE BRIDLELESS
  By the end of the book you will have tools to help you successfully transition your horse and yourself to a life of bridleless riding.

- A BASIC OVERVIEW OF HOW TO USE POSITIVE REINFORCEMENT TRAINING
  You will learn some of the basic principles of positive reinforcement training which you will need along the way. I don't go into great detail (maybe that's another book!) but I'll give you enough to start out and use it to transition under saddle to bridleless.

- A DREAM FULFILLED
  I'm assuming you are here because bridleless riding is a dream of yours and I can tell you that if you use this book in the way it's supposed to be used then your dream will come true and you will be ditching the bridle before long!

- A LAUGH AND A GIGGLE
  Horse training should be fun for both horse and human! If it's not then what is the point? One of the reasons I married my husband was because he made me laugh so I've tried to make this book a bit of a laugh to allow you to release some of those, 'feel good' hormones along

the way - just like your horse does during positive reinforcement training.

What you WON'T find is:

- THE SCIENCE AND PHYSIOLOGY OF THE TRAINING
  I will include a tiny smidgen as it is useful to understand what is happening during training with positive reinforcement, but my aim is to make this a fun, easy to read, simple and practical guide that appeals to all ages. There are a few other books on the shelves that do go into the science so you can pick them up separately if you want to get into how the horse reacts at a deeper level to positive reinforcement training. There are no big scary words, just simple, practical advice.

- RECOMMENDATIONS FOR BITS, WHIPS AND TIE-ME-DOWNS
  I train in an ethical way using the L.I.M.A (least intrusive, minimally aversive) principle so that means you won't find any advice on how to whip your horse, how to strap it down or how to scare it into submission by whacking a rope on the floor or tapping it with the end of a carrot stick. It's all about making the process enjoyable for the horse so that he wants to participate.

I've divided the book into two parts:

1)   THE BASICS OF POSITIVE REINFORCEMENT TRAINING

For those of you who are just starting out with positive reinforcement training or have no idea of what it is or how to incorporate it into training with your horse, I'd advise you to start at the beginning of the book. You will find the very basics of the training, exercises that you can teach your horse and everything you need to know to set you and your horse up for success on the ground. Once you've worked your way through part one you will (hopefully) have grasped the basics which you can then take on to stage two with you.

2)   HOW TO RIDE BRIDLELESS WITH R+

For all of you R+ pros, you can recap the basics and see if you pick up any new things along the way or you can just go straight to part two where you can begin the bridleless training. Here you will learn how to start teaching your horse the basic cues from the ground and there is a step by step method that will enable you to not only stay safe in your transition but also to fulfil that dream of stripping the bridle from your horse's face and riding calmly without one.

The Horses in this Book:
I've had the privilege of meeting and working with many different horses over the years and as you work through this book you will hear about some of them. I've included case studies and my personal experiences and I felt I should tell you a little about them so you understand the context of where they have come from.

Bella
You have already heard a bit about her. She is a chestnut Anglo Arab who is now 26yrs old. She lived in a huge herd before she was backed at 4 years old. At 5 years old she threw her rider

and bolted but ended up colliding with a wall and losing the top of her ilium. She had months of box rest but came through it. Understandably she hates to be stabled; she hides pain well and she is also to this day very particular about who she will carry on her back.

Tari

Tari came to me as a 3yr old who had only been taught basic husbandry tasks. She is currently 6yrs old. She would resource guard with food and she had a habit of biting. She bit the vet during her vetting; she bit the gardener when she arrived and she bit my husband. She has been trained with the clicker from the very beginning of our journey together from the ground to ridden work. She is no longer a biter!

Amber

Amber is a hillpony-x-arab who I took on a year ago having previously worked with her for a year before that. She was unhandled, had deep rooted fear and I suspect P.T.S.D. She'd had foals taken from her and aversive training was not successful. Her progress is slow with the clicker but it is progress all the same. She is learning to trust, and we celebrate the small steps.

The wildies

I work for a charity who take Hill ponies in, handle and train them before finding loving homes for them to live out their days. Most come in completely frightened and untouchable, and any human contact has usually been of an aversive nature.

Client horses

Some of my clients have very kindly allowed me to use their horses as case studies throughout the book, so the odd one or two will be mentioned.

SAFETY:

I guess safety has to be the first place to start in this book. To many people, the idea of riding a horse out on the lanes and across Dartmoor with nothing but a rope around the neck is a reckless thing to do. I have received some backlash and criticism for what I do and my reply is always the same: 'I trust my training. Just like some may train a horse to respond to a bit and pressure off the legs, I train mine to respond to voice cues, seat and cordeo. Bridleless riding isn't just about what the horse is or isn't wearing on its face, it's about the rider looking at a variety of other factors which we will cover as the book progresses.

DISCLAIMER:

I have to say at this point that, if you're based in the UK (and possibly other countries), you won't be covered by your insurance company if you do choose to eventually ride out bridleless , but I believe we all have lines that we draw concerning risk. There are lots of riders who wouldn't ride bitless; there are some who won't jump a 3ft fence; there are some who won't go hunting and there are others who wouldn't lead their horse at liberty from the field. We all do things everyday with our horses that put us at risk. We take a calculated risk the moment we decide to sit on a horse. No matter what you choose to dress your horse in when you get on its back, the most important thing is that you put the correct training in place and listen to your horse so that you know that in most circumstances your horse will listen to the training. The training that comes along with this book takes a holistic approach which I believe also adds to the safety of the horse and rider. I actually believe it is no riskier than any other part of our horsemanship if we take this approach.

THE LINGO IN THIS BOOK:

There might be certain words in this book that you have never heard before so I'm popping this here so you have an understanding of what I mean.

AVERSIVE

Something that the horse finds undesirable

BRIDGE

A noise or word that is made before a treat is given. The click tells the horse that the behaviour is right and a treat is coming.

CAPTURING

Marking or clicking a behaviour that happens naturally. This takes patience! For instance, if you are looking to train your horse to lay down then you might have to sit in the field with him until you spot him going down. When he does then you have to be ready to, 'Click' and reinforce.

REINFORCE

Reinforcers or reinforcement can come in both negative and positive terms dependant on whether we want to see more or less of a certain behaviour. When I refer to it in this book I mean we are adding something positive after a behaviour to make that behaviour stronger.

STIMULI

An object, person or place that evokes a response.

PART ONE: THE POSITIVE REINFORCEMENT PART

Chapter one: What, Why, WOW!

CLICK...ER WHAT?

If you picked up this book and haven't dabbled in positive reinforcement before then don't worry: I'm going to teach you the very basics. We aren't going to go deep into the science of it all, since you bought this book to learn about how to ride bridleless, not to have to endure a two hour science lesson. I think we can all safely say that we were pleased to leave that behind the day we walked out of school, threw our books in a raging fire and laughed like a scary witch during the process....oh that was just me? Well, ugh hummmm.......moooooovving on!

R+/POSITIVE REINFORCEMENT/CLICKER TRAINING? I'M CONFUSED!

During this book you'll see that I refer to all three of these names. Basically, I'm just trying to confuse you wildly before you start, in the hope that you will get so confused and frustrated as you go that in the end you won't bother reading the book. No that's not it at all of course! I did think that it might be easier if I stuck to one name but most people who use this type of training don't, so I figured that if I use all three you will become familiar with them. Next time you are reading a post on Facebook you'll then realise that they all mean the same thing in terms of training. The only thing I will say though from my own personal perspective, rightly or wrongly, is that the phrase 'clicker training' is used more by people who engage in trick training or who are adding this type of training to their repertoire, whereas people that use positive reinforcement training embrace the training holistically so it's more of a lifestyle and it runs through everything they do with their equine. Finally, R+ means positive reinforcement but it's the written language that most behaviourists will use to describe it.

WHAT IS POSITIVE REINFORCEMENT TRAINING?

Unfortunately, the equine world is so far behind in terms of the use of positive reinforcement training. The most common way of encouraging a horse to learn in the equine world is either by positive punishment i.e. a whip to the butt or negative reinforcement i.e. waving a rope at a horse until it moves out of your space.

Many zoos and animal centres have been using positive reinforcement for years because they realised a long time ago that asking or motivating an animal into a desired behaviour rather than forcing it is much more enjoyable, ethical and safe.

The definition of positive reinforcement is where something added increases the behaviour. So, for example, teenage son Noah's bedroom is such a pigsty. You've been holding back for weeks as your little hands want to get in there and not only clear the floor space so you can actually walk on the carpet but you desire to give it a massive deep clean as you are fretful that a group of trolls may have moved in and made themselves a home. One Sunday afternoon you decide to venture inside and pick up some clothes to wash for fear of him having nothing to wear and having to run around the countryside with his bare butt on show for all to see and to your surprise as you open the door, not only are you met with a smell that resembles a male aftershave section in the mall, but the whole place is immaculate and little Noah is stood sporting a smile that would not look out of place in a Colgate advert. When you've had a minute to marvel at the wonder before your eyes you tell Noah how wonderful he is for what he has done and then tell him he can have an hour or two on his computer. You reward Noah for

17

the desired behaviour that you wanted to see with some time on his beloved computer and wonder if he loves the computer more than he loves you. On a serious note, Noah has been rewarded and with something that he finds highly reinforcing and the chances of that behaviour (the cleaning of the room) occurring again is very high.

WHY WOULD I TRAIN THIS WAY?

    a)   It's science based.

I know, I know, I said I wasn't going to get into the science but bear with me! Well besides it being enjoyable and fun for both yourself and your horse, clicker training is based on science and the physiology of the horse. It activates something called the seeking system and 'feel good' hormones like dopamine, unlike when we use punitive methods which activate the fight/flight system and in turn releases stress hormones such as cortisol. If a horse is in flight mode then it is fearful and fear inhibits learning, but I did say I am not going to go into the science in this book so I will stop there.

    b)   It gives the horse a voice.

Another reason to train this way is because it also gives the horse a choice and a voice in its daily living. Quite often as horse people we make every single choice for the horse. We tell it when it should have a bucket feed, when it should have a rug on, when it should spend time in a stable, when it should be ridden or lunged and even if and when it can go out and play with its friends when in the horse's very ethology, it needs its friends to survive, to feel safe, to feel comfortable with life itself. We take away just about every choice from that animal with what we think is best for it and is best for its welfare, but what if we could open the doors of communication to a whole new level and let our horse decide some of these things?

Let's take the average horse: the rider wants to exercise the horse on the lunge, the horse doesn't get a choice. They start out in a headcollar with the lunge line attached. The person tries to direct the horse in a circle to the right but the horse just wants to come and be with the person. The person then thinks that the horse just isn't getting it so picks up a whip and waves it around which worries the horse, so the horse starts running around in a circle to get away from the whip. The horse relaxes a little and slows down but the person waves the whip around again, so the horse worries and speeds up with its head in the air. The person doesn't want the horse to run around with its head in the air so they decides that they should put the pessoa on so the horse to brings its head down. What the person hasn't realised this whole time is that the horse is talking but the person doesn't understand much - like how I would feel if I went to China.

With positive reinforcement training we can give the horse a voice. It might look like this:

Me: 'Hey horse, would you like to walk this circle with me?'

Horse: 'I'll come over and see what this is all about'

Me: 'Thank you for joining me **(click)** and here's a treat for making a good choice'

Horse: 'Ohhh that was nice. Maybe if I just follow..... you..... around...... like......this'

Me: 'Well done! (click) and here's another treat because you walked half a circle for me'.

The conversation goes on until the horse is walking a full circle and then trotting a full circle and then cantering all without sticks, ropes or any kind of force. You just give the horse a choice in what he does but have rewarded the behaviour you wanted to see. It's the difference between being asked to do something rather than being forced to do something. It's the difference between choice and no choice at all. I know we can't give choice all of the time. For instance my horses would love to be on luminous green pasture all of the time and that choice really wouldn't be good for them because they'd get fat, sick and unhealthy, but if I can use R+ and put the ball in their court for 90% of our interactions then that makes for a better relationship all round.

Chapter two: Tools of the Trade

There are a few things that you'll need before you can get started on your journey with positive reinforcement.

CLICKER

A clicker is a little device like the one in the picture that makes a loud noise when you press the button.

You don't have to use an actual clicker though: I don't a lot of the time because a lot of my training is done with feral ponies that have just come in off the moor. The clicker would scare them off once and for all so I use a gentle 'click' of my voice. Some of my clients might use the word, 'good' because the horse has had an aversive past and has been pushed on with multiple 'tongue clicks' so they want to get rid of that sound altogether. It's entirely up to you what you use. You just need to use something to bridge the gap between you seeing the desired behaviour and reinforcing with a treat or scratch. The reason for this is very simple: it helps with timing. You need something you can action instantaneously so you can tell your horse exactly what it was that you were happy with and then your horse will learn that the treat is on its way. If we don't use the bridge signal then by the time you reach into your treat bag for a treat, move into your horse and allow your horse to take it from your hand, your horse could be doing a completely different behaviour altogether and may mistake that behaviour which you are trying to reinforce.

TREAT BAG

You need somewhere to put your treats. Lots of trainers

will use bum bags or over the shoulder bags, or you can even buy silicone pouches that sit on your hip. Take your pick! You will see as you continue to work through this book that it really is about finding what works for you and your horse. The main purpose of the treat bag, aside from holding the food, is that it is easy to access so that you can get your hand on a treat as quickly as possible so it gets to your horse's mouth soon after you have bridged.

I personally don't use a swanky bag but instead I have very big deep pockets in my hi-vis waterproof coat which not only hold a lot of treats but also enable me to get my hand in and out without it getting stuck along the way. On the one day a year in the UK where it isn't raining or cold then I have a shiny bum bag that my mother in law bought me.

TARGET STICK

Whips, carrot sticks or lunging ropes are used in traditional horsemanship in an aversive way by hitting the horse across the flanks or waving it at the horse to get it to go in the direction that you wish it to go. Whilst we do use whips in positive reinforcement training, we don't use them in an aversive way. We never hit the horse. We build a positive association with the whip by transforming it into a target so the horse isn't scared or worried about it (this is particularly important if your horse has had a bad experience with the whip) and then we can use it to entice and engage the horse.

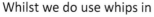

A typical target might be a long whip with a tennis ball on the end. I actually use an extendable feather duster. We can also look at using stationary targets like a traffic cone, and these work particularly well for fearful equines who find a stimuli being presented and moved around a little too worrying. You'll learn more about targeting a bit later on but in the meantime take your pick as to what you might use.

REINFORCER

The reinforcer is simply a posh name for a reward or something that you give to your horse after the bridge. This is something that the horse chooses because it needs to motivate it enough to want to train with you so  it's down to you to figure what is rewarding for him or her. Some trainers use food and I find for the most part this is what works best for most equines. Some trainers use scratches. You can also choose to use your voice and I find for certain equines they really do respond to your tone of voice. For some horses you can see their eagerness grow as you really praise them for what they are doing. It's almost like their faces light up. I use a mix of the three as they all work, dependant on who you are working with and what time of the year it is. For instance, when the horse's coat is coming out then scratches are high on the list of reinforcement and if a mare is in season then they tend to like them too. Food and praise work well as a stand-alone or combined.

It's really up to you as the trainer to find which one works best for that particular horse.

Case study- Millie

Millie was a little anxious pony whose person asked me to come and help with her. Millie's person had found out about clicker training and had started using it to help Millie settle a little. On

23

my arrival I could see that Millie was very wary of me and kept a watchful eye on me from the other side of the yard as her person and I chatted about her background. After a short while she did come over and greet me, and I could see that life in general was scary for her. As our lesson progressed her person was using food for the most part when she used the clicker but every now and again, she would say, "good girl" and give Millie a nice scratch on the neck. Each time this happened Millie would tense up a little; the whites of her eyes would show and she would turn her head away or take a step away. Even though Millie's person was trying to use scratch as a reward, Millie didn't see it that way. It was aversive to her. Once I'd pointed this out to Millie's person, we worked on other ways that we could positively reinforce Millie and change her mindset towards the touch.

Chapter three: All About Food

I know some people struggle
with the idea of using food to
train horses, but every single
living being is driven by food. I
mean, why do we work a job?
To get paid so we can eat and
pay the bills. Horses are
designed biologically to eat for
 a whopping 18-20 hours a day, unlike the majority of us who
eat 2-3 times a day for an average of 15-30 minutes. Food is
high on a horse's list of reinforcers so why not use that to our
advantage?

WHAT FOOD SHALL I USE?

It really is down to your horse and it's up to you to figure out
what works for him. I use a mix of things dependant on who I
am working with. Again, you have to find out exactly what your
equine prefers that keeps them within threshold (I will touch on
that a little further in a minute). So, if I'm working with a pony
that is fresh off the moor then I find hay or haylage is enough of
a reinforcer for them and then I might move to a low molasses
chaff. If I'm working with my pony then hay cobs are our
standard choice but I throw in carrots here and there to keep
her interested. My youngster finds carrots too exciting, so I just
use hay cobs for her. My old mare engages with carrots, hay
cobs and hedgerow plants. So, you see, you have to figure out
what works for the horse that is there in front of you.

If the reinforcer is too HIGH then it is likely that your horse will
go over aroused. This means that they typically will get bargy or

snatchy, maybe throw the head, or their facial muscles could become tight.

If the reinforcer is too LOW then you may find that the horse loses interest and walks away, or they won't display the behaviour you are asking for and they will seem generally disinterested.

JACKPOTS

Don't worry: I haven't suddenly got my wires crossed and am about to tell you how to succeed at the casino. This isn't the type of jackpot that pours dollar from the fruit machines. A jackpot in the positive reinforcement world means that you give your horse a nice big handful of really high value treats. This is usually given after they have performed a behaviour that you deem to be worth a big 'well done'.

Case study- Amber and jackpots.

I'd been working with Amber for months and months around her fear of ropes. Initially I couldn't bring one onto the yard without her scarpering, so when one day she decided to stick around and then actually touch it with her nose, I dumped a huge pile of carrots on the floor for her as this was such a huge step forward for her. This was a jackpot moment.

HEEEEEEEYYYYY! GET OUT OF MY POCKET!

One of the pitfalls with positive reinforcement training is that people tend to encourage the horse to come to them when they are retrieving a treat. They will fiddle in their bag, pull out a treat and then keep their hand by the bag or by their body. The trouble with this is if you feed from the pocket, treat bag, bum bag (or whatever you choose to carry your treats in) then the likelihood is that your horse will bring its head to you to take the treat and he may not leave. You are then left with a horse that is sifting through your pockets and gets distracted by the other treats that you have on you and before you know it you're being eaten out of house and home or you're having to push your horse's head away from you. What you want to encourage is for your horse to be standing calmly, head facing forward and waiting on delivery of the food from you. You can train that and we will look at that later in the book but one of the ways you can help this is by always bringing the food to them. A great way to do this is by taking a treat from your pocket or pouch,

extending your arm out to in front of the horse and feed. You don't want the horse's head anywhere near you or you will end in an ever-frustrating cycle of grabby horse distracted by food smell in the pocket. I've been there and done that! It's not something that you want to fall into. If your horse does go for your pocket then you can go back to protected contact  (another thing we will talk about in upcoming chapters) for a while or I find stepping away from them and reminding them of a head forward, with the vocal cue "head forward" is helpful. It can be difficult if you are coming from a traditional background to not physically manoeuvre the horse's head with your hand, since that is usually what we would normally do. Old behaviours are hard to break right? Maybe we need some cakes in our own pockets so we can reward ourselves for desirable behaviour …ummmm!

You might find that the horse or pony you are working with isn't really that confident in how to take a treat. For instance, the wildies go through a little phase of having to learn to take them from the hand and it's all a bit fumbly and tentative until they become more confident. It tends to roll from the hand onto the floor and then they suddenly find their confidence and go the other way, becoming overzealous and practically taking your hand off in the process. The latter is usually a sign that the horse is over threshold or that the horse simply just doesn't know how to be around food. Another reason for this may be that your rate of reinforcement is too slow, so make sure you check out the bit about that in this book. In the meantime, here are a couple of ways to help you with food delivery.

THROW IT DOWN

Throwing the food into a bucket or onto the floor will sometimes help process become smoother. Be aware that if you are switching from treat in hand to treat into a bucket that this might confuse your horse a little in the beginning. What usually happens is your horse will naturally come to your hand because this is where it has learnt to pick up the treat previously, and you might get some frustration in the form of tight faces or even grabby teeth so the trick for this transition is this: At the start of your training session drop the treat into the bucket and then wait for your horse to find it. Eventually your horse will learn that the noise of the treat hitting the bucket means he should go to the bucket. The great thing about treats in buckets is bringing their head down also helps the horse to stay calm as certain endorphins are released as the head is lowered.

USE A SHALLOW DISH

A shallow plastic dish can be used to give your horse the treat but be sure to allow your horse to get used to this first before you start thrusting it in his face. Worry might overcome the need to take the treat.

PRESENT THE BACK OF YOUR HAND

Put the treat in your hand, make a fist and then stretch out your arm and present the back of your hand first before turning your hand and opening it. This works really well because the horse expects the treat but quickly realises that there isn't one as they lip your hand and in that moment you can present the treat.

I'M NOT FAT, I'M JUST BIG BONED
If your horse's weight is a worry and you need to be mindful of what is going into his mouth then don't worry, you can still use positive reinforcement with food. Here are a few methods that still enable you to train but help keep the calories on the down low!

1. Use hay. Obviously this will be down to your horse. If he isn't motivated by it then it's not going to work but it's worth trying.
2. Use his bucket feed.
3. Use low calorie fibre cubes. Something like Thunderbrook hay cobs are perfect for this.
4. Fill your treat bag with the amount of treats you are happy for him to have that day and once they are gone, they are gone. Training session over!

Chapter four: Protected Contact

WHAT IS PROTECTED CONTACT?

Don't worry, I'm not expecting you to go out and buy a suit of armour and a sword to protect yourself during training. Protected contact simply means that you are on one side of a barrier and your horse is the other. You can use a gate, a stable door, a piece of electric fencing and a couple of poles or even a pole resting on a couple of traffic cones. Again, just like the reinforcer and marker, you get to choose what is right for the horse you are training at the time. Be creative with the facilities you have!

WHAT IS THE POINT OF PROTECTED CONTACT?

1) Well, for a start it sets your horse up to succeed - especially in the early stages when you first start training with positive reinforcement. They are still learning this new way of training with you, the boundaries around food and what is expected. If you are anything like I was when I first started training with positive reinforcement then you are trying to figure it all out too. You're working on timing, fiddling with treats, dropping them on the floor as you try to reinforce, and getting your hand stuck in your pocket as you try to pull them out. There's so much to think about! It can be messy on both ends so if you do have any issues with getting the treat to the horse after you have marked the behaviour, then your horse won't be on top of you making the whole thing even trickier. As your horse learns what you are asking and you learn to be a bit smoother on your part then you can experiment without protected contact.

2) It gives you the ability to walk away without your horse pursuing you. Again, when you start training in this way your horse has to learn when a training session starts and ends and what is and isn't acceptable. If you are working with protected contact and your horse doesn't quite understand the behaviour you are asking for but instead is in your pocket and getting frustrated because he can't get a treat, then you can just take a step to the side to avoid being mugged.

3) I find that protected contact is a god send for fearful equines. There is a visible barrier between us that creates a safe place for them which helps them to be slightly bolder during a training session. Their fear is so prevalent that even coming into the stable or onto the yard where they are can be too much for them and their endocrine and neuro system start to automatically take them over threshold and set off the stress response in their body which is what you don't want when practising positive reinforcement. Keeping the stress levels as low as possible is so important, and protected contact helps us do that.

4) Aggression is usually exhibited out of a place of fear, so naturally it can come out if an equine feels threatened. I would always recommend using protected contact for equines who exhibit this behaviour, regardless of whether they are exhibiting mild aggression or severe aggression. It not only helps to keep us safe but it also does the same for the horse.

Case study-Tina, Midnight and protected contact.

Tina and Midnight were two elderly ponies estimated to be in their late 20's. Midnight was blind in one eye and before long it became clear that Tina was her carer. I don't think I've ever seen a more bonded pair. As soon as you entered the yard Tina would quickly start circling around Midnight to protect her and then round her either into the stable or a corner and stand to guard her. I knew that if pushed too far, Tina would feel forced to fight and I didn't want to put either of us into that situation. Human presence was highly stressful for the two of them so I avoided going onto the yard in the first few days as much as I possibly could, aside from throwing hay down and filling water. Initially it was even stressful if I was within 10 metres of the gate so I gave them both the space they needed and it wasn't long before the distance between us lessened and she relaxed with me being at the immediate side of the gate. Had I have not been using protected contact then I may have been hurt and the process of human/horse contact may have been far more stressful for the two girls.

SHOULD I ALWAYS USE PROTECTED CONTACT?

You can phase protected contact out as soon as you feel the horse is settled around you and the food source you provide, and I have to say that I don't always use protected contact from the start. For instance, my lovely old mare never goes for the pockets and never pushes her head into me to try to forage for the food. She just isn't the 'muggy' type, most probably because she has been punished in the past for exhibiting that sort of behaviour.

It really is down to you, the trainer. Go back to the idea that runs through this whole book. Look at the horse you are training, decipher his character and individuality and listen to him.

Chapter five: Setting up to Succeed

A lot of people try training using R+ but then give up because their horse gets bargy or tries to raid their pockets every time they enter the field or stable. Well, like every training path you choose, there need to be foundations laid down in order for the horse to understand the basics and when you do that and don't mar the lines of training then the horse very quickly picks up what is asked of them.

Before you start a training session it's good to consider the environment around you. What you want to achieve is as much freedom of choice for the horse.

LEAVE THE HEADCOLLAR OUT OF IT!

Ideally at this stage it's better for the horse to be at complete liberty: no head collar, no lead rope, no cordeo. For some horses even the very act of having a headcollar on their face is enough to shut them down a little as they have learnt that the headcollar means containment. It means they must demonstrate a certain action or behave in a certain way. With my old mare I only need to put a headcollar on her and lay the lead rope across the gate and she won't move an inch because she thinks she is tied up. She's not been tied up in the 10 years that she has been with me, yet she still won't move an inch when that lead rope is draped over the gate. Our desire is to allow the horse to have complete and utter choice without restriction so they can express their true voice. We don't want the horse to have any of these mental restrictions. We want him to come and go as he pleases, expressing his true voice throughout the training you do with him.

"I'M HANGRY", SAID THE HORSE

It can be really tempting to work with your horse when they are hungry - especially if you are in the early stages of positive reinforcement training and your horse might be saying, 'No', to you a lot, but I really would advise against this. For a start you aren't getting a true 'yes' from your horse, because if a horse is hungry then it is likely to push itself over threshold or over its limit of comfort, to get to the food. You will probably also find that the horse you are working with isn't fully relaxed, but is instead grabbing at the food and showing an array of stress signals as they are more focused on the food rather than the behaviour you are trying to train. It's important to give the horse real freedom of choice and that means a full tummy before you start training. It also means that hay should be freely available at all times during your training sessions so they can top up their tummies as you go if they need to. For some horses you will find that they like to opt in and out of the training sessions as you go and will get great comfort and relaxation from standing at a hay pile and eating for a short while. It also means that you can lay treats next to it at the end of your session and allow them to munch in between your sessions.

It is worth bearing in mind that even if a horse is at pasture with all the grass they could ever wish for, they could still be hungry as grass at certain times of the year won't provide the nourishment and fullness that a high fibre source like hay will provide.

PLACEMENT OF TREAT BAG

It's really helpful for your horse to place the treat bag away from him so he's not tempted to follow his nose and end up sifting through it. If you are stood at his left shoulder then just swing your bag around to your right side so you act as a barrier.

Similarly, if you're stood at the right side then swing your bag around to the left. If you're in front of him then slip it slightly behind you.

HEY BUDDY!

When we are working with our horses, we want them to be in the most relaxed state possible because they will learn more effectively. For most horses this will mean that they have other horses around them or at least in view, so try to make sure you work in an area that offers this. It's better not to have other horses loose as I usually find that the horse you aren't planning on working with smells the food, hears the munching or generally wants to engage in the behaviour training and then this creates conflict and resource guarding between the two. The best thing to do is to split the field or yard so that you have a space for the horse you are training on one side and the rest of the herd can potter around and watch what is going on from protected contact. I actually find it amazing how much other horses will pick up as they observe a training session. For some horses they will only need to watch and they will start offering up the same behaviour as they have seen a positive outcome; a treat.

TIMING

One of the most important things when using clicker training is your timing. When I say 'timing' I mean that you have to mark or click the behaviour at exactly the right time. Too soon or too late and you risk training something that you may not wish to train. It's always harder to un-train a behaviour than to just get it right in the first place. No pressure! Haha! I'll expand on what I mean. Imagine you are training your horse to lift its leg on cue. You ask using your already trained voice cue, your horse lifts but as it's bringing the hoof down it paws the ground. If you don't 'click' when your horse has its leg in the air, bent backwards towards the hind end but instead 'click' a little later as your horse paws the ground, then congratulations: you are training him to paw the ground! It's not such a big deal if you do this once or twice but the more repetitions with the wrong timing and your horse will most likely end the leg lift with a paw. I once accidently trained my youngster to bring her head towards me when I haltered her and then her nose ended up in my treat pocket and there was a struggle: it was just this ongoing thing that frustrated us both, all because my timing was off and instead of clicking when she put her head in the halter, I must have clicked when her head was in and turning towards me. This undesired action became part of what she thought was the sequence of behaviour that I so desired from her. It was a mess and it wasn't something I was even aware I was doing until my horse started to show me.

The great thing about clicker training is that it is possible to retrain something although it's best to try and not get yourself into that pickle in the first place since helping a horse to change learnt behaviour is much harder than training from a fresh slate.

So timing is really important but the only way you will improve is by putting it into practice. It can be super helpful to practise with a family member or friend before you start working with your horse. If no one is keen to work with you then use the power of positive reinforcement to change their mind:@)

RATE OF REINFORCEMENT

Rate of reinforcement or ROR simply means how often you 'click' and reinforce. If you are teaching a new behaviour or have a fearful pony then it's important to keep the ROR at a high rate delivering lots of 'clicks' and treats in a small timeframe. As the horse understands what you are asking and builds confidence in that behaviour then you can start to slow the ROR down.

SHORTER IS BETTER

It's really tempting to think, 'Right I have all day free, I'm going to go up the yard, bring my horse in from the field and just spend as long as I can teaching and training him so he will progress quicker. He will learn so, so much and he will be carrying me bridleless, rearing on cue, walking down steps, allowing the dog to ride him and sitting on cue before the end of the day'. However, research suggests that long drawn out training sessions get you no further along the training than if you do just a couple of short sessions each day. When you train for long periods of time the information in the middle of the training quite often gets lost as the brain can't process it all. It's better to keep your sessions short and consistent.

TINY PIECES

During training we always need to be mindful of the fact that we want to make the behaviour as simple as possible for the horse to understand. The best way

of doing that is to break the behaviour you want to teach into tiny pieces. Think of a puzzle: some have two pieces, some ten pieces, some have two hundred and some have thousands. It depends on the ability of the puzzler as to what size puzzle you might attempt. You wouldn't give a two-year-old child a 1000 piece puzzle. It's the same for our horses. We want to break it down into as many tiny pieces as your horse needs. If you are trying something easy then your puzzle will only be small but if the behaviour, the end result, is complicated then your puzzle needs to be bigger.

For instance, if I'm teaching a neutral head behind protected contact, which is a foundational behaviour I would consider a simple behaviour, most horses pick it up quickly so my puzzle would be small.

 The horse would be behind protected contact

 My pockets would be full of different treats

 I'd stand and capture when the horse puts its head exactly where I would like it to be and 'click' and treat him at that point.

 I'd add in a voice cue: "head forward" and 'click' and treat when my horse responds.

Puzzle complete!

If I was going to teach a horse who fears being ridden through a river, then it would go something like this (although some of these pieces would have to be broken down even further and become a whole separate puzzle in itself like for instance if your horse didn't know how to long rein then you'd have to teach it):

Teach to move leg on voice cue, tarp, puddle, stream, leat, long rein, ride

 Ask horse to stand on tarp, up onto a step, into a puddle using that voice cue only. Clicking and treating every step of the way.

 Go to a slow flowing shallow stream and ask horse to walk through with you at his head whilst clicking and treating him. When the horse is confident move onto..

 Go to a faster flowing shallow stream and ask the horse to do the same again. When the horse is confident...

 Long rein your horse through the shallow stream with a person at his head clicking and treating until confident.

 Long rein your horse through a shallow stream without a person at his head until he is confident.

 Ride your horse through both the slower and faster flowing rivers.

 Go to a fast flowing, deep river and walk through with him whilst clicking and treating.

 Long rein him through the deeper river whilst clicking and treating.

Hopefully you get the picture, or should I say puzzle? Hahah! You may not need to break it down this small or you may need to break it down even smaller for the horse you are working with. I personally find that it is better to break it down smaller to start with and lose some puzzle pieces down the back of the sofa than end up with missing pieces to start with or you may find that you push your horse too fast and then have to go backwards.

WHERE'S THE START AND FINISH LINE?

When you first start to use R+ training, having a definitive start and a definitive end to your training sessions is one of the biggest things that people tend to miss and yet it is in my eyes one of the most important. I teach this in the very foundations of the training because this can not only cause the horse the most confusion and frustration, but it can be the trainer's biggest reason to give up on R+. Have you ever waited in a queue to get some food and found out when you get to the checkout till that they are no longer serving? Its frustrating right? If you don't have something in place that tells your horse when you start and finish training then how is he supposed to know when snacks are available or not? What often happens is that people skip this part and then complain that they have a muggy, rude or pushy horse, but he is only like this because he has learnt that treats are available around the clock. If you skip this phase then there is more chance of your interactions being negative as you deal with a frustrated and potentially dangerous horse.

HOW DO I START AND END A TRAINING SESSION?

WEAR SOMETHING

One of the best ways of letting your horse know that you'd like to work with him is by using what is called a discriminative stimulus. It's a definitive object that you might wear or present at the start of the session and remove at the end. Some like to use a bum bag or treat bag, or a bright scarf that is easy to put on or off. As long as it stands out then get creative. If you've always wanted a reason to buy that multicoloured fluffy tutu then now is the time!

SAY SOMETHING

As you will see as you make your way through the book, vocal cues are so powerful. At the beginning of each session, if the horse doesn't come running when they see me or when I've put on my discriminative stimuli then I might say "Would you like to play?". I have this beautiful clip on my Facebook page of me working with Amber at a stationary target, with Stumpy tucked away in one of the stables where neither of us can see him, helping himself to some hay. After a couple of repetitions with Amber, I say "Stumpy, would you like to come and play?" and he appears and joins in with us. The power of the voice.

LEAVE SOMETHING

Your horse needs to know that your training session is over for now but if you just decide you are done and start to walk away then your horse might find this punishing since you are leaving with the food. There is also a risk that he might follow you in frustration and this could compromise your safety. The best and most effective way to stop this from happening is to end your session by saying, "All done" and popping a big handful of whatever is in your training pouch onto the floor next to the hay and then walking away. Your horse is left eating his treats which is a nice thing for him and you've ended in a positive way. If you are unable to walk away then whilst he is eating the treats and hay you will have time to take off your fluffy, pink tutu and your treat bag and pack it away in the tack room with your feather duster!

END ON A HIGH

Ending on a positive note is always how we want to conclude our sessions with our horses, meaning that in both of our minds we are left with a good experience rather than left remembering the bad. It's up to you as the trainer to make sure this happens, so if your horse is struggling with a particular task or you get the sense that you've pushed your horse a little and he is feeling worried then go backwards to an exercise that he knows well and loves to do. Ask him to do that a few times, reinforce lots and end it there.

Chapter six: Listen to the Horse

HOW DO I UNDERSTAND MY HORSE'S LANGUAGE?

Horses are speaking all of the time. They have a language that we humans are yet to fully tap into but at this point in time we understand it a little. Just like if we were to move abroad and didn't speak the native language, we would make an effort to learn it so we could understand the people better and they could understand what we are communicating, we need to do the same for our horses. By making an effort to learn their language, we can better facilitate their life in this modernised world that we expect them to live in and help keep our horses and ourselves happy and safe.

When I go out to see a horse after a big behavioural incident like bolting, rearing or aggressive behaviour the horse owner will often tell me that 'it came out of nowhere'. I often hear that 'the horse was absolutely fine and then.....' or 'it's like a switch flicked in the brain, like he's got some sort of mental problem'. After talking through the incident in the owner's own words and observing the horse myself, I can generally say this really isn't the case: the horse was speaking all the time in the lead up to the incident, but its voice was missed in the process.

One of the biggest factors when using R+ training is being mindful of your horse's emotional state, and the best way to do this is to learn about stress signals, thresholds and body language. There are many books that go into this on a deep level so I'm only going to touch on this subject but I do recommend that once you've read this book to go off and read up some more as it will open up a whole new world in your relationship with your horse.

BODY LANGUAGE AND STRESS SIGNALS

If a horse is starting to feel anxious about something, he will release little signals that help him regulate that stress. They are known widely as calming signals (but I prefer to use the term stress signals as I feel it explains more clearly what they mean), appeasement behaviours or displacement behaviours. These behaviours start off subtly but will progress as the horse goes up the ladder of fear.

So if a horse is anxious you might see things like:

- Whites of the eye showing
- Licking and chewing
- Yawning
- Excessive eye blinking

If their anxiety progresses then this can lead to stronger stress signals like:

- Rubbing the face on the leg
- Turning head away from the stimuli that is making them anxious
- Sniffing the ground
- Shaking the neck/head

If the stimuli or something in the environment continues to really worry the horse then this can lead to:

- Pinned ears
- Walking/running away (if the horse is able)
- Pawing the ground
- Presenting the hind
- Calling out/being vocal
- Rearing up
- Biting
- Kicking

- Pooping excessively

Once again, it's so important to gauge the horse you are working with and understand what is normal for them. This is merely a guide and some horses will have a higher threshold than others based on their life experience and character and one horse may go over threshold way quicker than the next horse. Use these pointers as a guide not as gospel. Every horse is different.

Case study-Bella and the way she speaks.

Bella is my old mare who I have had the pleasure of knowing for 10 years now. She speaks in some interesting ways - ways that others may not understand if they didn't take the time to get to know her. For instance, when we are coming to the end of our ride and go past a certain tree, if she would like me to get off and walk with her then she will go and stand under the tree so my face is in the branches and that is my cue to dismount. She learnt to speak in this way after she did it once and I dismounted, she did it again and I dismounted. She realised that by standing there, I would get off. If the average person was riding her and she started to edge towards the tree they may well mistake her language for bad behaviour and punish her for it. When considering some of the signals above if she is left alone then she will very, very quickly start to poop a lot, vocalise and run around with her head in the air. If she sees a horse box then her facial muscles will become tight and she will give it a wide berth whilst turning her head away and licking and chewing.

THRESHOLDS

My son loves to drum, but he doesn't always use his drum kit. He will bang his hands on the sofa, he will bang on the table, he will bang on his legs, he will bang anywhere. When he does it I don't even notice at all yet my husband will tolerate it for a short while and then suddenly get to the end of himself and ask him to stop. It really gets on his nerves for some reason. In the head up to him vocalising his stress, he will glance at my son, he will blink lots, he will shift in his seat and tap a foot. You can see that it's really bothering him until he has to verbally say something to try to stop this thing that is causing him stress.

We all have thresholds of how much we may or may not tolerate a certain thing, and it's the same for our horses. Each horse will have a different threshold and that threshold can differ from one day to the next dependant on factors like how much sleep they may have had, how hungry or thirsty they are and how much they have been able to move. That's why we might hear horse owners say things like:

"He had no problems walking past those cones in the street yesterday"

Or

"She was fine yesterday but today she is so grumpy! Look at those ears"

Well, maybe, just maybe your horse didn't get much REM sleep last night, or perhaps your mare is coming into season and her hormones are affecting her mood. We all know how that one feels, hey girls?

It's up to us to learn what that individual horse's limit is and keep them way below it but at the same time also help them to learn to stretch that limit whilst changing their mindset. What makes them worry and how can I help with that? What can they deal with on a minor level without exploding? What are they marginally happy to do? What do they thoroughly enjoy doing?

When we work with horses we understand that they are living beings. They have that flight or fight instinct within them, so we therefore have to be mindful of their reaction to their environment and the stimuli within that environment. All horses react differently to different stimuli on different days dependant on how they feel about it and what memories have been stored in the brain so it's really important to get to know the horse you are working with and know where they are at with these things. Horses go over threshold if we don't pay attention and when they go over threshold they will fight, flight or freeze or fiddle about. We want to try avoid all of these, especially if we are working towards bridleless riding.

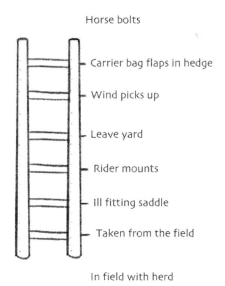

Horse bolts

- Carrier bag flaps in hedge

- Wind picks up

- Leave yard

- Rider mounts

- Ill fitting saddle

- Taken from the field

In field with herd

Take a look at this ladder. You can see that every rung represents another thing that worries the horse until he just isn't able to hold it together any longer and off he bolts.

COMFORT ZONES

When we are working with our horse it's up to us to gradually and carefully stretch their comfort zones. If we push too much then we risk creating fear within the horse and crushing their confidence, and if we push too little then the horse doesn't reach its full potential and its confidence doesn't grow. Take a look at this comfort zone seesaw. If we overload the horse whilst training behaviours, we risk taking him too far out of his comfort zone. We need to closely monitor the horse to ensure they do not become overloaded and fearful. It's a fine balance which is why it is so important to pay full attention to those stress signals, body language and thresholds.

Comfort zone

Case study- Bella being ridden out in a group

I offered to take a group of lovely ladies out on a hack as they didn't know the local area. It was a beautiful day and I was really looking forward to it. I took Bella from the field knowing that she hadn't been ridden for a couple of days. Stack one! As I tacked her up, she could see all of the other horses on the yard being tacked up. These were horses that she didn't know. Stack two! There were about four or five horse boxes on the yard and Bella has a real fear of horse boxes. Stack three! We were the first to be ready, so we had to wait around for the others while they finished getting saddles and bridles on their horses. Bella is a horse who doesn't like hanging around once she knows we are off out. Stack four! When everyone had mounted we started off up the drive and Bella was miles out in front feeling quite stressed out. I thought she might calm down as we got going but then another horse tried to overtake her and that was it, she wasn't listening to me at all. Stack five! She was jogging sideways and was dripping with sweat all within being five minutes up the road. It was then that I had to opt out of the ride and leave the ladies to fend for themselves. Bella was already way over threshold and I knew one more thing and we would be bolting off into the unknown.

Chapter seven: A Few Things to Bear in Mind

ALWAYS HAVE A PLAN BUT BE PREPARED TO DUMP IT

I don't know how many of you have given birth but prior to having the baby, you will be given a sheet of paper where you have to write down your ideal birthing plan. On it you write the things that you would like in terms of medication, where you would like to be at the time of the birth and who you would like to have with you. This piece of paper is your 'Ideal' and when you are a first-time mum, this piece of paper means a lot. You have these high hopes of sticking to it word for word and isn't until you experience labour that your 'ideal birthing plan' starts to change a little...and then a lot and then before you know it, you are screaming out, "Give me the flipping epidural" when all you wanted was to meditate and pray to the Lord as the baby came through the birth canal into a world of peace and laughter. It's the same with the training sessions with your horse. No I don't mean that you have to give birth to your horse, I mean you might have to go in with your 'ideal' training plan but be prepared to be flexible because so many things can affect how the plan might work out including and not limited to the environment, your emotional state, your horse's emotional state and many other factors. Meeting your horse where she is, is so important as an R+ trainer.

Case study-Tari and a change of plan.

Tari is my 6year old Arab who has been trained with positive reinforcement since she came to me three years ago. It was very early into her ridden life that I made a loose plan the day before to take her off the farm for a little hack around the village but we would start with a couple of exercises on the ground that she knew well. This would progress to a sit on her back whilst on the farm and then eventually we would leave the farm for our hack. When I went to the field to greet her, it was particularly windy and the herd were all on high alert but I still tacked her up and we played around with a few of the planned exercises. As we did this it was clear that she was struggling to concentrate, although she did settle down and focus once we ran through all of the things that were familiar. It was during this process that I decided that riding out for a little hack needed to be aborted since she was already stacking, and hacking out with a rider was fairly new to her. We continued with some groundwork and eventually ended up at the mounting block which is a particularly lovely place for her since we have used a high rate of reinforcement there from the very beginning of our journey together. She relaxed a bit more and I found myself onboard and we had a little ride around the farm. I know that had I stuck to the plan then she most probably would have gone over threshold and who knows where we would have ended up? The last thing you want with a newly backed horse is a negative experience.

So have a plan but more importantly tune into where your horse is emotionally minute to minute and go from there. Sometimes you stick to the plan, sometimes you change it a little and sometimes it goes completely out the window, but the main thing is that you are focused in on your horse and listening to what she was saying.

Another reason to have a plan is because it sets your horse up for success. Imagine that you go into your training session. You've set up the environment for success with your hay freely available, your target is at the ready and your horse is willing. You start with a bit of targeting and that's going really well, you ask for a back up which your horse does beautifully but then you stand there and wonder what you should train next. Your horse is waiting on you to give him his next cue and you aren't sure. The seconds tick by and your horse offers up a random behaviour that you have previously taught him but he isn't getting reinforced so he moves on to something else but again he doesn't get reinforced. He starts to show signs of frustration by pawing at the ground or head shaking which means he is starting to stack. He steps toward you and you are still unsure of where to go so he goes for your pocket and you step away from him. He does it again and then you end up pushing his head away manually with your hands. As you walk away your horse nips at you and what started out as a really positive experience, ends up being punishing for the both of you.

Imagine that you go into your training session with a shaping plan instead. The whole process has much more flow because you know in your mind that if your horse achieves behaviour A and behaviour B then you can move on to behaviour C which has already been broken down into little achievable pieces. You end the session on a high and everyone is doing a happy dance.

I'VE STARTED DOWN THIS ROAD AND...

- Everyone on my yard and beyond thinks I'm crazy!

Yes they do my dear and unless things change overnight in the horse world then it's something you'll just have to live with.

Years ago horse shoes didn't make sense to me so I got them taken off my mare's feet; I didn't like how she responded to the lump of metal in her mouth so I rode without it. Eventually I realised I didn't always want to ride my horse so I'd take her out walking so she could peruse the hedgerows and we'd arrive back at the yard with a saddle sporting lots of different plants for her to enjoy. I was on traditional livery yards where the internet wasn't like it was today and I was a complete novice who lacked confidence in my own abilities. I had people questioning what I was doing, why I was paying so much money to treat my horse like a pet and people would tell me that what I was doing was an accident waiting to happen. I didn't really have what I felt was a good enough answer for my decisions, but I knew my horse appreciated it. Currently I live in a village where very few people understand the way I train horses; where I walk the lanes with a bunch of treats in my pocket and a bright pink fluffy feather duster in my hand. I am sure the way I train gets questioned and if I'm honest, I probably would have questioned it myself too some years ago because I look like a crazy lady who fails to see that a feather duster should be used around the home not around horses!

Whilst positive reinforcement is growing, in the equine world it's still not as prevalent as it could be and when something is new, it can be scary. When fear surrounds something, people can be judgemental about it and that is a lonely road to travel if you are on the receiving end of that judgement. As with everything you must believe that what you are doing is right for you and your horse or you will be pulled down by the naysayers (or should I say neighsayers!) and the judgement from others. If you are the type of person who likes to have an answer, then clue yourself up on the science behind this way of training so you have a response for those people. The great thing is we have the internet and there is a growing trend of people out there in the wider world training with positive reinforcement so get involved, join some groups where you can see that others are doing it too and you are not alone and feel connected. That's what I've had to do because if I look at just my little village and the little villages beyond then I am alone with this lifestyle. There are not many people here waving their feather duster with pride as they parade the streets. You have to be prepared to stand alone, just do what you do and hope that people get curious and see that the way you train isn't this whacky thing with no substance to it.

- now my horse hates me!

Sometimes if you have a horse that is really shut down or even a horse that has a mildly aversive past and then you suddenly start to give them a choice in what they do they realise that they can say 'no' and some say it really, really, really, really loudly. You go to the field and find that they run from you instead of to you like they previously did. You try to pick up a foot to pick out the hoof and your horse won't move an inch. You go to put the saddle on and your horse scoots to the side and wiggles around like a snake. This is normal behaviour and you just have to be prepared to give your horse the time it needs to adjust and come onboard. Some horses are just so beaten down by their past or by having no choice at all that it becomes super scary when they realise that they are able to use their voice, and sometimes it takes them a while to find it. What usually happens over time is his mindset starts to change. He realises that time with you is time well spent (I mentioned dopamine earlier - well, your horse will start to feel good when he sees you and interacts with you because training with R+ releases dopamine into his body). Instead of having to walk to your horse to catch him in the field, he actually sees you and comes bombing it down, that you can just say "up" and he will lift his dear little leg for you and will line up in front of you when he sees his saddle.

- This is really hard.

Yes it is! You are learning a whole new way of horsemanship and that's not easy, but you've got this! Learning any new skill is difficult and if you've been doing horses for many years then it's going to take a bit of time for you to take in new information, for your brain to reshuffle, chucking out the old stuff and rewiring the new. Go easy on yourself and in the same way as I guide you to train your horse in this book, take some of those principles for yourself too. Maybe don't go and stand by yourself at the mounting block and feed yourself sweets and chocolate, but do break things down into small pieces so you don't get overwhelmed with the bigger picture. Keep your learning sessions short. Reward yourself with something that you like doing inbetween your learning. Go easy on yourself and try to enjoy this whole new world that is opening up between you and your horse.

Chapter eight: Exercises

GETTING STARTED ON SOME EXERCISES

Here are some simple exercises that you can start teaching your horse so they start to understand what the clicker means. These exercises also help you get to grips with what you are doing before you take to the saddle.

1) STANDING CALMLY

Standing calmly is the place I like to start with any horse. For some horses when you start to bring food into the mix it can send them over threshold - especially if you have a horse that was a rescue or has been used to running out of food on a regular basis. My youngster took a long time to realise that food was always going to be available because she'd quite often run out of hay in the stable before she came to live with me, so for her this exercise was difficult to start with.

How to teach it:

 Have your horse in protected contact.

 Stand beside the barrier and carefully watch your horse.

 When your horse is chilled out and stood with you calmly just click and reinforce.

It's as easy as that!

Problem solving:

My horse never seems to relax or appear calm

- Rule out pain. A horse who can never relax may be in some sort of discomfort.
- Keep your sessions short. Look for one or two signs of calmness and end it there. Eventually she will work out what you are reinforcing for and you'll see more of it and be able to reinforce it more.

If that doesn't work, then:

- Look at your environment. If you are trying this exercise in the stable and your horse doesn't like a stable, then you are setting the horse up to fail. Take your horse to the paddock and set up protected contact there, but if your horse gets anxious when other equines are around then make sure that you put a divider in so he's not constantly having to think about resource guarding you and the food you carry. Just figure out where he's most comfortable and then work with him rather than have him fit into your box.
- Wait and have patience. The chances are your horse will be the most relaxed when he's out with his mates in the field. Just hang out with him and when he looks relaxed reinforce him once, lay some treats on the ground and walk away. Keep doing this and then you can go back to the previous step as he becomes more relaxed.

Case study-Serena

Serena was a moor pony who was completely wild. Any interactions she had with humans were aversive until she arrived with me. She was actually a really quiet girl, but I noticed early on that she would go over threshold when food was offered. She would push into me, her ears would go back and she would throw her head around. She would try to grab my pockets and her whole face would tighten up. For a long time, I allowed her to just be, to settle in, but eventually the time came when I needed to start working with her so that the charity I worked for could get her rehomed. In the beginning I started working with a vocal click and very low value treats, but she just got so easily aroused that I went back to working with hay. I did try haylage which initially worked with her but unfortunately over time she lost interest in it. Hay soon became a similar story and she really wasn't bothered so I ended up using some low value hay treats for her. We had to keep the reinforcement really high and for a long period I only used hay treats over protected contact, working on standing calmly and a head forward. When I did eventually start working with her without protected contact I had to keep our sessions super short so I would ask for a behaviour, she would offer, I would 'click' and reinforce, then we would repeat and I'd end the session. If she was my own horse then I would have spent a lot longer with her on how to be calm around food and worked over protected contact and on our relationship for as long as she needed, but she had a home lined up so this just wasn't possible.

2) HEAD FORWARD

The second foundational exercise you want to train is a head forward or a neutral head. This means that the horse's head is facing forward. It's not in your pocket, it's not thrashing about all over the place, but your horse is nice and calm with its head out in front of him. Most horses find this exercise really easy once they realise what you are reinforcing for and it's a great way to get started. It not only sets them up to succeed in an exercise but it's a simple one for you as you start out and it helps your horse get used to what the 'click' actually means.

How to teach it:

 Start in protected contact.

 Stand with your back to the horse, shoulder to shoulder.

 When your horse is stood with his head forward then click and reinforce.

 Add in a voice cue: "Head forward".

 Keep going until your horse fully understands the voice cue and will respond accordingly to it.

 Take away the protected contact and see how your horse responds. If he's in your pocket then he hasn't quite got it yet or he needs more help with impulse control. Keep working with protected contact before you move on.

Problem solving:

- My horse just mugs me.

The advantage of starting behind protected contact is that you can step away if your horse starts to mug you or get fractious. Simple! The mugging stops because you are no longer there to be mugged. Wait and then catch the head forward, 'click', and reinforce. Your horse will soon understand what he's being clicked for.

- My horse is thrashing its head about all over the place and I'm worried I may have turned him into a head shaker.

The easiest way to stop this is to up your reinforcement rate. As soon as your horse's head is in that neutral position, 'click' and feed, and keep feeding. Work on your timing. When your horse understands where his head needs to be to get the treats then you will find he will do it more often and eventually you can slow down the rate at which you give the treats. The behaviour has to be marked as soon as the head is forward and always in the same position.

If you struggle with your timing on this one then you can start by using a visual target stick. A target stick? I hear you ask. Read on to find out more!

3) TARGETING

Targeting is a brilliant exercise to teach the horse and I've used it in all manner of situations to help horses through different experiences. The idea with targeting is that you train the horse to hit the target with his nose (or other body parts) and you can then go on to ask your horse to follow the target. You use it to encourage forward movement from the front rather than pushing from behind with a whip or a stick or a rope. It's also a brilliant confidence builder/security blanket for the fearful or worried horse.

I love the way that targeting can change the whole mindset of the horse. He might be worried about that wheelie bin or that signpost but as soon as I ask for them to "target" and point at it, the horse recognises the request and all of a sudden the stimuli isn't scary anymore and over he walks to touch.

I will start by teaching you how to nose target but you can teach the horse to target with any part of its body.

How to teach it:

 Stand by the side of your horse so you are shoulder to shoulder and pop the target stick in front but not on his nose. Be careful not to suddenly bring it out of nowhere at a rate of knots or you'll scare him. Work slowly.

 Usually the horse will explore it with his muzzle and when he does you just, 'click', pop the target out of view and then reinforce.

 Introduce a vocal cue like "target" or "touch" as you present the stimuli.

Problem solving:

- My horse is too scared of the target

If your horse is worried about new stimuli then pop the target stick on the ground and let him explore it at his own pace. Be sure to 'click' and reinforce any advances he makes towards it and when he touches it too.

- My horse grabs the target in its mouth

Some horses are super mouthy and will really get involved with the stimuli so this is where timing comes in. We don't want to reinforce for the bite so the trick here is to 'click' on approach rather than wait until it's too late and the horse is already biting.

- My horse won't interact with the target at all!

Some horses are sadly shut down especially if they have had an abusive past so there are a couple of things you can do in this situation

1) Leave the target somewhere where the horse can see it. If you notice any interaction with it when you are around then you can 'click' and reinforce that.
2) Continue on with the other exercises and have a think about what different things you could use for a target. I have a pony who is really fearful so presenting a target stick to her just wouldn't have worked so I started simply by asking her to touch my hand.

Case study-Tari and the target stick

My young Arab Tari and I were out on one of our walks when she was really young. We were walking the moor, it was fairly windy and she saw a horse and rider cantering in the distance. She started to go over threshold and I knew that if I didn't help her then she could well be joining them with me running like a loony behind her trying catch her so....out came the target stick as a distraction. As soon as she heard the word 'target' and I presented our bright pink fluffy duster, her attention was back on us and what we were doing. We ran through some of the basic exercises that she knew and carried on with our walk.

4) HEAD DOWN

When a horse lowers its head, he gets a release of endorphins and hormones that help him to relax so it's a really powerful exercise for horses who struggle with calmness and fear.

How to train it:

There are two ways you can go about training this. I will give you both and you can see what works best for the horse you are working with.

PUZZLE ONE

 Once your horse is trained to the target then lower it to the floor and when your horse touches it simply 'click' and reinforce, whilst removing the target.

 Add in a vocal cue, "head down" and again 'click' and reinforce whilst removing target.

 To add duration ask for the head down as before but delay before clicking.

 You can get rid of the target with this exercise when your horse recognises the voice cue "head down". Ask with the voice cue and if your horse doesn't respond then he doesn't quite understand the voice cue yet. Keep repeating.

PUZZLE TWO

Puzzle two uses body language rather than a target, which I find works better for horses who are fearful.

 Slightly bend at the hip and point to the floor.

 On any sign that your horse shows of lowering the head, 'click' and reinforce dropping the food on the ground.

 Wait for the head to come back up again and repeat.

 Add in a vocal cue: "head down".

Once the horse understands then you can slowly phase out the bending at the hip, just using the point to the floor.

 You can then slowly phase out the point by not being so obvious with the point, by keeping your arm and hand closer to your body.

 Ask with the voice cue and if your horse understands then he should respond by lowering his head when he hears you say "head down".

CASE STUDY: Bertie and the head down

Bertie was a horse who would go over threshold quite quickly so I knew that teaching him a, 'head down' would really benefit him especially when we started to expand his borders within his immediate environment. He very quickly caught on to the exercise and once he realised the benefits of the positioning of the head for himself as the hormones raced through his body and calmed him, he found it so reinforcing that he didn't even take a treat. After a while he would naturally go to a, 'head down' after a stressful event and just stand there in a daze.

5)   HEAD UP

I know that many equine enthusiasts find nothing more frustrating than walking or riding through a field of grass where the horse is stopping at every whipstitch grabbing for grass or worse still, the head goes down and you are stuck there forever as the horse gorges on the green stuff. Well, this cue is invaluable for riding and for bridleless riding in particular since there are no reins attached to the face so even if you wanted to, you couldn't pull them off the grass.

How to train it:

If you have a horse who finds the grass really tempting and won't come away from it for love nor money, then you are going to have to find a reinforcer that is of really high value to him, higher value than the green stuff! I'd also recommend training this in the winter when the grass isn't so sugary and sweet as your horse will find it easier and not be so tempted by the green stuff. Hopefully by the time the summer does come and the grass is in full swing, your horse will have developed the muscle memory for this exercise and respond to your cues.

I would recommend training this OFF the grass first and with a full belly so your horse can learn the cue. I've given you an option here with the target stick and without but YOU CAN MIX AND MATCH. Just choose what works for you and your horse. I'm like a broken record!

OFF THE GRASS WITH THE TARGET

 Pop some hay on the floor and wait until your horse is eating.

 Present the target stick a little above the horse's head and say "head up".

 When the horse lifts his head to touch the target stick, 'click' and reinforce.

 As your horse start to understand then you can raise the target stick higher.

 Practise without the target stick once you are confident that your horse knows the 'head up' cue just by voice.

ON THE GRASS WITHOUT THE TARGET

 When your horse is grazing, wait for them to take a pause. Be patient. Some horses take longer than others! As they raise their head, 'click' and reinforce. Repeat this numerous times. Again, being patient is the key.

 Add in your voice cue and keep on repeating.

When you are in the saddle you can add this final piece to your puzzle.

 Lightly squeeze with both legs whilst using your voice cue and immediately release regardless of whether your horse listens or not.

6) GRAZE

It's also useful to train a cue so your horse knows when it is acceptable to graze. This one comes in very handy when you are out without a bridle. It's best to train this on the ground first.

How to train it:

 Point to the grass and say "graze" (or whatever cue you choose) and when your horse goes for the grass just 'click'. He's reinforcing himself by eating the grass so you don't need to feed from your hand.

Hopefully your 'head up' cue is working well by now so when you are ready to leave the grass, your horse will respond to that.

PART TWO-THE BRIDLELESS RIDING PART

Chapter nine: Before We Start

This is exciting right? You are just a few steps away from fulfilling your dream but more importantly, entering a new realm of riding that opens up a whole new door of communication with your horse. Before we start with the training there are a few important things that are worth pointing out when it comes to riding bridleless.

OUCH!

There is something you should know that is really important! *Puts on best teacher voice* AHEM! A cordeo CAN HURT YOUR HORSE AND IT CAN CAUSE DAMAGE! Imagine if someone popped a rope around your neck, stood behind you and then pulled with as much strength as they had in them. Well not only is that going to hurt but it's going to send you into a coughing frenzy and feel like you are being strangled. The horse's trachea runs from under the chin to halfway down the neck and if the cordeo is placed too high it can interfere with breathing. If you have that cordeo up under the chin or are yanking it hard then of course your horse will go where you ask it to because any impact from that rope is going to hurt so they will work to avoid the pain. The idea of bridleless riding is to create a light communication with your horse and if he isn't listening and you feel the need to pull hard, to move the cordeo up the neck so you have more control, then you need to look at retracing the steps in this book. Just because there is no bridle it doesn't mean that hands tugging and flapping about all over the place can't aggravate, hurt or interfere greatly with the horse. There! I will put my teacher voice to bed and continue.

You can see in the first pic, which was taken recently, that I am barely touching the cordeo. It is hanging loose, touching the chest, there if I need it and if other communications fail. In the second pic. which was taken a few years ago, my hands are heavier, gripping the cordeo with both hands and if you look closely, whilst it's not super tight, it is interfering. It's worth noting that even though I am gripping the cordeo, it's still low down on the neck near the chest.

I am of the mindset that the neck rein should really be the last port of call rather than the first. There are many steps before the cordeo comes into play. If your horse doesn't listen and you find yourself not only using the neck rope but applying heavy hands OR you need it so far up the horse's neck before she takes note of what you're asking then please reconsider going back to groundwork and training.

PLACEMENT OF YOUR HAND

When it comes to riding with a cordeo you can forget everything you learnt in your riding school days. The pinkie finger thing does not exist here. Let the cordeo hang loose and with the top of your hand facing skyward, use a pincher grip to hold it where your horse's mane sits. If your other fingers are feeling left out and you feel more comfortable with a loose cupped hand over the top of the rope then do so. For every communication through the rope your hand stays here.

ENVIRONMENT

Remember at the very beginning of this book I spoke about taking a holistic view on riding bridleless? Environment is a huge part of that holistic view. When you do decide to throw the bridle then you really have to be aware of how your horse is reacting to the environment around it. You know yourself that you might ride in the arena one day and your horse is totally happy yet on the following day he is spooky and reactive. For him the environment changes each and every day and being a flight animal, we have to be in tune enough to read our horse's voice before deciding to take the bridle off. Remember those stress signals that we spoke about in part one? They really come into play here! If your horse is going up that ladder then choose another day to take the bridle off or perhaps change your plan a little and ride but with the bridle on using the cordeo. Far too often the rider will blame the horse for its reaction which is totally out of the horse's control when the responsibility actually lies with the rider. The horse is a flight animal and if threatened, whether we personally see it as a threat or not, the horse will generally want to get as far away from that threat as possible. We have to be able to look at our horse and not only see if it is coping with the current environment but put things into place so that it can cope.

Here are some good questions to ask yourself before choosing to take the bridle off:

Is my horse in familiar surroundings? If not, then how does he usually react to unfamiliar places?

How is my horse feeling now? What stress signals is he giving off? How's his body language?

Case study: Bella

When I was retraining my old mare to bitless and bridleless, it was all going really well. She was listening to everything I was asking of her. Our stop cue was on point without any rein pressure or any cordeo pressure - just voice and seat. One day we were out riding with a friend and her horse and we were coming home from a lovely two hour hack across Dartmoor. The horses were very aware that we were nearing home and had a spring in their step: Bella generally likes to get back to her herd when we've been out without them. My friend and I were yapping away totally unaware of what our horses may have been thinking and we decided we should have one last canter. As soon as we said the word our horses obliged and then neither of us could stop them. I have to say at this point that I was bitless and the other horse was bitted. Neither of us had any control because our horses went over threshold. Had I have not been too busy chatting then I would have noticed that both horses were on the verge of being over threshold and would have decided that at this point a canter was not a good idea. Since this experience if I go out with other riders then I won't allow myself to disconnect from Bella. I always make sure that I'm aware of her state of mind.

GENERALISING

Following on from the environment section I feel I must include a small part on generalising. Just because our horse can ride bridleless in the arena doesn't mean he can do the same whilst out hacking, and vice versa. You might find that you can jump a clear round in the arena with no tack and he responds without even having to use the cordeo yet whilst out and about, your horse is a little worried, a little anxious, a little fearful which means that you might find that you need to work on his

71

confidence whilst out hacking before you throw the bridle. Again, it's being mindful of what your horse is communicating to you and respecting that.

THIS IS SCARY!

Going bridleless can be scary for some horses, depending on how they have been ridden before, which is why it is so important to make sure you are training your horse so that he feels confident without the bridle.

Some years ago when I was a bit naïve and (I'll admit) didn't quite know what the hell I was doing (secret: I'm still learning and will continue to do so as long as I encounter horses), I was working with a young horse who had been backed quite young and then ridden in quite a strong bit, a martingale, draw reins and the reins were always tight regardless of whether he was stood still or flat out gallop. I worked with him for a bit and then decided to see how he would respond to riding in a cordeo. I dropped the reins and asked a couple of things from him but he was so overwhelmed at actually having his head that he took off at high speed in a frenzy. You see he relied so heavily on tight reins that they had become his security blanket and this is quite often the case for horses who are ridden this way.

Even when you pull the bridle from the horse's face and they are used to being ridden on a loose rein bitless, they may still feel a little insecure at this change

If you are working with a horse that has been ridden in this way then the first step is to slowly start to loosen off the reins when you ride. Give your horse its head even if you start for a minute or two each ride and build from there. An important part of the journey is for your horse to learn that he can feel safe and be independent, despite not having his face held, but if you follow the steps that are about to come then you will teach your horse how to feel safe and independent.

ALL ABOARD...OR NOT!

How does your horse feel about the mounting block? Is he happy to stand unaided while you mount or does he do everything in his power to evade it? If a horse is unhappy about being mounted then it's our job to rule out pain, consider whether there are any other reasons why your horse might not want to be ridden and then you can look at the training side of things. If you are going to ride your horse bridleless then you need to be sure that your horse is more than happy to stand while you carefully get onboard. This is a prerequisite to any of the training that is about to follow. It's essential to make the mounting block a fun and rewarding place to be.

REINFORCE! REINFORCE! REINFORCE!

When your horse responds to what you ask him to do either in the saddle or on the ground it is really important to use the principles of positive reinforcement mapped out in part one of this book. If you ask for a stop with your voice and the horse does it, then reinforce with the thing that he finds

Tari after she has just been reinforced for stopping on cue.

most reinforcing! The more you do this, the more of a muscle memory it will become so you will get to the point where your horse will respond automatically as soon as you either use your voice, use your voice and stop cue, use your stop cue and cordeo.....you get my point?

DON'T BE AFRAID TO GO BACKWARDS IN GOING FORWARDS

I know so many riders who go through the process of backing their horses or training them from the ground and then it's almost like they forget about that part as they progress into ridden work. When things go pear shaped with their horse, they see it as a massive step backwards if they have to pick up the groundwork again. I am a 'recovering perfectionist' so I totally understand this but my day to day work with horses, particularly wild horses, has seen me constantly taking three steps forward and five steps back. It's not failure but it is a key part of the process and it's completely normal. What tends to happen is you will go back but then you'll go forward and slightly push past the point you were at before. Then you might go back a little and again move forward and again go past the point you were at before. So, in going backwards you are moving forwards. If you have a mishap then just get off your horse and go right back to the ground. Your horse hasn't forgotten what you have taught him; the chances are he is reacting to his environment or his own physiology and it's up to you to assess his thresholds, look at what he is telling you and then re-trace.

Chapter ten: The Mounting Block

So, where do we start with bridleless riding? Well I believe that there are a few main components that you need to train the horse in, to not only take your horse bridleless but to do so safely. By the end of this section you should have the individual tools that can be used alone and together to ride well, and if you're anything like me then you'll appreciate a visual at this point. I like visuals: they help me to learn and...erm, visualise.

So, picture the mounting block. Most yards have them. I don't myself; I tend to make use of any grass verge, hedgerow, or lump and bump I can find to climb aboard my trusty steeds, but most people have some sort of method which involves stepping up or perhaps even jumping up (if you are one of those people who I'm totally envious of that can jump gracefully on board). Regardless of what we use, when we stand to start our ascent to the block, where are we? Well, our feet are on the ground aren't they and that is exactly where we start our bridleless journey, with our feet fixed firmly on the ground.

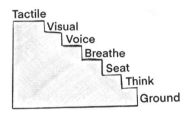

GROUND

Oh the dreaded 'G' word that no one really wants to bother with! I hear your voices ringing out in unison, "Stuff that! Let's just jump on board and go for it!". You could do that if you like but you might well disappear into the sunset or end up in the mud so listen up homie: the ground is where it's at! When you start on the ground you not only get a good gauge of where your horse is with whatever it is you are trying to teach them, but you are less likely to be injured, hurt or thrown if there are kinks in your training that need to be ironed out. This is where it starts. This is where the magic happens!

What you want to do is to start using the cordeo as you work from the ground, so your horse begins to get used to the feel of it and the fact that when he is working with you, the halter isn't always going to be on his face. As I said before, for some horses the halter is security, so by using the cordeo on a daily basis, that will become more of a security for him and he won't be freaked out when the halter comes off.

Rather than go and bring your horse in with a halter and lead rope, bring him in with a cordeo and lead rope. As your horse moves it will get used to the fact that when you go left, the right side of the cordeo will respond and when you go right, the left side of the cordeo will respond. When your horse heads out too far in front of you the cordeo will automatically respond to the chest area and when he is with you the cordeo will simply hang there.

When we start on the ground and teach the horse everything it needs to know from there, then when we finally sit ourselves on our horse's back what usually happens is that the horse knows exactly what it's doing and more importantly is confident with what is being asked despite not having you in its eye line. The confidence in knowing what he's doing isn't reduced, even though he can't see you.

MIND

When I say use your mind, I'm not asking you to start humming and going off into this meditative state for hours and hours with your horse (although meditation is good). I just

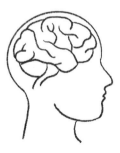

mean think about where you want your horse to go and what do you want your horse to do. You've probably heard people say similar things to, "Oh I just thought I'd like to have a trot and my horse trotted. She read my mind". Whilst I do believe our horses are finely tuned into us, I don't believe they can read our minds in the literal sense. I believe instead that the horse responds to the subtle changes in our body as our brain links to the body and tells it to prepare it for our next move. As a rider it's not possible to be thinking 'trot' without perhaps sitting up a little, shoulders back and moving our lower leg. The horse will learn to notice these cues and act accordingly.

SEAT

What do I mean by 'seat'? I don't just mean your butt cheeks. I mean your whole body. Being aware of where your legs are, where your shoulders are, what you are doing with your head. Now I'm not embarrassed to admit that I'm not very self-aware in terms of my body. I went to a dance class once or twice and I  did those keep fit classes where you have to all go in sequence with each other to the beat of the music on a promise that you'll lose weight and get fit. I'd always be the one going in the wrong direction, one step behind everyone, sweating like a good'un and looking like a complete fool. My idea of dancing is the sidestep and that's as far as it goes but I can tell you that riding horses has really developed my self-awareness because I have to use my body to ride. When you don't rely on the reins anymore like my eleven-year-old former self, then you use other things to signal to your horse where you would like it to go. If I'm not in balance, then neither is my horse and I'm throwing him off. If I'm looking to the left but want my horse to go to the right, then my horse is most probably going to go to the left.

BREATHE

Breathing is a vital step in the mounting block analogy, yet it is so underrated. It really is so powerful when working with horses and the great thing is you don't need to remember to take it with you when you are out with your horse, but 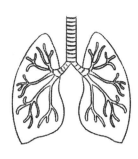 you do need to remember to use it! We've probably all been there, where we are in the saddle and the horse gets a bit reactive to something so we get a little worried and hold our breath or inadvertently speed our breathing up which makes the horse more reactive and before you know it, you and your horse are a quivering mess. Yet if you remind yourself to breathe deeply and focus your mind then it can have big impact on both of you. I find for myself that if I am worried in the saddle then I forget to breathe and every now and again take these big gulps of air in automatically because I'm not breathing and getting enough air into my body. If you don't breathe then your body is tense and vice versa and your horse will feel that.

VOICE

The voice is another tool that is a highly underrated addition to the horse trainer's toolbox. I'd say that both VOICE and BREATH are intrinsically linked since you can't use your voice without breathing. One of

the valuable things about our voice is it helps us to breathe and in turn relax. I haven't taken much from my traditional riding lessons from my childhood, but one thing that I have carried on with and hold value in is to use my voice when I ride. My instructor taught me to sing 'Twinkle, twinkle little star' if I was feeling worried or if my horse was getting wound up and it would work like a dream at getting us both to relax. One of the most embarrassing moments of my life was when I was out riding and belting Adele out at the top of my lungs and around the corner came this old couple. Rather than just making a joke about it we all just trundled past each other awkwardly not acknowledging what had just happened. I quite often sing to my horses because they find it calming and of course it helps me to breathe. The voice is a wonderful tool. We can raise it a little, change its tone, speak a little louder and when your horse learns to pair a voice cue with a treat, well something wonderful happens. They listen and they respond.

This is another tool that tends to disappear when we are worried in the saddle.

VISUAL

Using a visual cue when you first start is really helpful in just adding another element into the mix to help your horse learn what you are asking of him and set him up for success. Remember the puzzle piece analogy I was talking about earlier? Well, this is just a way of giving bridleless riding another piece of your puzzle, breaking it down a little further for your horse. A visual is easier from the ground dependant on what you are trying to teach but when you've got all of your steps in place there are some cues that I don't use a visual for and some cues that I do.

TACTILE

A tactile cue is the final piece of this puzzle. This is a cue that the horse can feel. This could be a slight gentle squeeze with the LEGS or a gentle 'ask' with the CORDEO that sits around your horse's neck. It's an important part of the puzzle that we want  to train but not rely on. By the time we get to this piece we should really have everything else in place so our horse already knows what we want him to do but the cordeo is helpful in giving a clearer picture to our horse if we feel he needs it. If used correctly then direction should be used lightly and in an unobtrusive way.

SADDLE

Congratulations you've made it to the saddle! This is where we finally get to put everything we have taught our horse into practice, where we take that all important final step into the stirrup and onboard our trusted steed and see if our ground cues transfer to saddle.
Before you throw the bridle and see if what you have been training your horse works, here is my suggestion. Keep the bridle on and practise a while. Put all your steps through their paces and see how your horse responds. Does he listen? How far up the mounting block do you go before he starts to listen? Are there things that you need to go

back to and perhaps get a bit more polished? If not, then now is the time! Chuck that bridle and give it a whirl.

Chapter eleven: The How To

How this works!

In this section I'm going to teach you how to teach your horse the cues you will need on the ground and in the saddle. I will use the simple concept that I have just explained; THINK, BREATHE, VOICE, SEAT, VISUAL and TACTILE. During some of the groundwork teaching it's not possible to use all of these steps - for instance the SEAT principle won't generally come into play - although sometimes gentle body language can be used so I may highlight that in places.

The idea with this section is to give you, the reader, all of the steps you may need to ride bridleless but as you and your horse go through this process and your horse learns each step, I hope that you will see that unlike the positive reinforcement training where you need all the pieces to complete the puzzle, here you really can play about on those mounting block steps once you've taught all of them and your horse understands them. If you can take just the first step on the mounting block and skip the rest then that's awesome! If you can step from the ground to the VOICE step then that's amazing! Teach all the steps and then have some fun! Our aim is to use as little as possible to engage our horse to listen. This is not an exact science. It's based on science but because your horse is an individual you might find that these steps need a little rearranging for your learner to understand.

STOP CUE

I always start with a stop cue. Ironic hey? I find it to be the easiest of all the cues to teach and this is the one that we want to be ingrained into the horse's muscle memory so deeply that it will work no matter what. The only way to do this is by going over and over and over it. When I say this I don't mean you should spend hours in one session repeating the same cue. If you do this then your horse will most likely switch off and get bored, or you might find he becomes satiated with the reinforcement and doesn't want to participate or worse still, he gets obsessive about this one cue and offers it up all of the time at random. Keeping the sessions short and doing a little every day will enable your horse to have time to think and most importantly, sleep on it and store it in his memories.

ON THE GROUND

STAGE ONE

 Have your horse with you at liberty, on a cordeo or in a headcollar. Whatever works best for that particular horse at that particular time.

 Take a walk together.

 THINK- Stop. Think about coming to a progressive stop rather than an abrupt stop. You want the transition to be smooth so think smooth stop.

 Stop moving and BREATHE in...and on your out breath use your VOICE and say 'whoooo-aaaaahhhhh'.

 As soon as your horse starts to slow down, 'click' and reinforce.

Move from clicking when your horse starts to slow onto clicking when your horse has two feet firmly still.

So initially you are rewarding the 'try'- the slowing down to make the whole thing easy and setting your horse up for success and then you are rewarding the actual stop.

When you think your horse has got this exercise move on to this:

STAGE TWO

 Walk with your horse.

 THINK stop but continue walking.

 BREATHE in and as you breathe out use your VOICE: "woooooo-aaaahhhh".

 When your horse stops, 'click' and reinforce.

If your horse can do this then you know that he has learnt the voice cue, rather than mirroring your body language.

When your horse is able to do this then move onto this:

STAGE THREE

 Walk with your horse.

 THINK- Stop.

 BREATHE in and as you breathe out, use your VOICE, "woooaaaaahhhhh". Use the CORDEO by gently pulling upward towards the withers and release. It's really important here to release the CORDEO whether the horse responds to your cue or not.

 'Click' and reinforce if the horse responds.

The idea with this exercise is not to escalate the pressure on the cordeo to get the horse to stop. You've taught him the voice cue so he should respond to it, and that is why when we add in a cue with the CORDEO, we ask and then stop rather than continuing to add pressure until the horse gives the desired behaviour. This is the major difference between positive reinforcement and negative reinforcement. We don't want to escalate the pressure, because we still want the horse to have a choice. If the horse doesn't respond then repeat the stage and if he doesn't respond multiple times then you know that you either need to go back to stage two as he clearly hasn't got the VOICE cue in place, or perhaps you need to look at thresholds and the environment.

IN THE SADDLE

 As your horse is walking start to THINK about stopping.

 Use your SEAT by leaning back a little.

 BREATHE in and as you breathe out use your VOICE by saying "Wooooaaaaahhhh".

 Gently pull back on the CORDEO and release.

 'Click', and reinforce when the horse responds.

DIRECTIONAL CUE

Obviously, direction under saddle is really important. I will use this part of the book to help you teach your horse to step to the right but exactly the same principles apply in the opposite direction. For the sake of setting your horse up for success I would suggest teaching one side at a time. Get out your feather dusters everyone! It's target stick time! Hopefully you have taught your horse to target your target stick by now because you're gonna need it!

ON THE GROUND

STAGE ONE

 Stand in front of your horse with your target stick hidden behind your back.

 THINK about which direction you would like your horse to go in.

 Present your TACTILE cue- your target stick, slightly to the right of your horse so he has to stretch his neck to reach it. As soon as his neck starts to go towards the target, 'click', reinforce and remove the target. Once he has done this a few times, move on.

 Present the target a little further to the right so he actually has to move his body. As soon as his shoulder starts to edge towards the target then you can 'click', reinforce and remove the target. Do this numerous times over various sessions before moving on.

 Present the target a little further away and this time you are going to be waiting for him to start to move his feet a little. Once he has done this a few times then you want to ask for a proper step to the side.

STAGE TWO

 Present your target to your horse and use your VOICE cue: "right". As he steps to the right then 'Click' and reinforce. Remove target. Repeat the process multiple times over many short sessions.

STAGE THREE

 Stand in front of your horse without a target and move your right arm outwards slightly and use your VOICE cue at the same time: "right".

 As soon as your horse starts to move towards the right then 'click' and reinforce. If your horse has difficulty with this then you can reintroduce the target again or stand beside them shoulder to shoulder and ask them to step right as you mirror your body language.

Once your horse is responding to your VOICE cue without the target you can move on to stage four.

STAGE FOUR

 Stand shoulder to shoulder with your horse. THINK, 'right'.

 BREATHE in and on your 'out' breath use your VOICE

 Gently take the right side of the CORDEO in your hand and lightly pull to the right and let go gently. 'Click' and reinforce when your horse responds.

Once your horse is able to take one step to the right then ask for another step and so on.

IN THE SADDLE

 THINK about going in the right direction.

Use your SEAT. Turn your head to the right and the rest of your body will follow.

 BREATHE in and on your out breath use your VOICE cue: "right".

 Use your TACTILE cue; gently pick up the right side of your cordeo, pull and release.

Once your horse is responding to all of the above you can add in a second TACTILE cue. In the same way that we do with the cordeo, by asking but without adding more pressure if our horse doesn't respond, we will do that with the leg cue.

 Use your second TACTILE CUE: leg. Use your left leg to gently squeeze your horse's side and release whether your responds or not. If your horse doesn't respond then squeeze again and back it up with your VOICE, VISUAL and TACTILE cue.

WALK ON CUE

There are multiple ways that you can teach a 'walk on' cue and I thought it might be helpful to include a couple because we all like choice just like our horses do right?

ON THE GROUND

METHOD ONE

This method includes the use of your target and has the prerequisite that the horse has learnt to bop its nose to the target and to have a strong reinforcement history with this.

Stand shoulder to shoulder with your horse whether that is at liberty or in a headcollar. Again, whatever works for you and your horse.

 THINK- forward.

 Present the VISUAL cue: the target, to your horse and as soon as the horse starts to edge towards the target, 'click' and reinforce and remove the target. It's important to keep the target still whilst the horse is reaching for it. We don't want to lure the horse as this can often create frustration.

 Gradually up the behaviour requirement for your horse. If he starts by reaching towards the target with his head then move the target a little further away so he has to move the front leg a little, then 'click' and reinforce for that. Move it a little more so he has to move both front legs to touch it and so on. Once this behaviour is fairly solid you can then move on to piece four.

 Add in your VOICE cue: "walk on".

Trying to keep your feet still during this exercise will help as your horse won't be copying your body language but will instead be going towards the target.

METHOD TWO

For this method you will need to set up an inside-out lunging pen. You'll need around 6-10 cones or some electric fence posts, maybe more depending on how big you want the pen to be. Place the cones or fence posts in a circle leaving gaps between each one.

Attach electric fencing and you'll end up with a small circular pen. In traditional methods of lunging, you'd have the horse in the pen and you might wave a rope at it or perhaps a whip and get the horse going from behind but we are going to motivate the horse to 'walk on' from the front end.

 Stand in the inside of the pen and invite your horse over to play. When he comes to you reinforce with food or scratches. You want your horse to be on the outside of the pen not inside with you. You can use your VISUAL here (your target) if you want to but I've found it works just as well with the horse mirroring body language.

 Take a step forward and as soon as you see your horse make any move forward, 'click' and reinforce. Repeat until you feel the horse is understanding.

 Ask for two steps and then three and so on. Eventually ask for a quarter of the circle before reinforcing, then half etc.

 Add in a VOICE cue.

 Now you want to start phasing out your own body language and this is the part where you see if your horse is responding to your voice cue or your body language. Use your voice cue and stay standing still. You can face in the direction you want your horse to go and look in that direction too.

If your horse doesn't respond, then you know you need to take your body language down gradually. Try demonstrating a step or a polite hand gesture in the way that you'd like your horse to go. If your horse is still struggling then go back to piece two.

METHOD THREE

This method is for all of you who are like me and perhaps forget a target when you leave the house; don't have the facilities to set up an inside out lunging area or who keep their horses on a yard where leaving cones and various other equipment around is just not allowed. You have to get a little bit creative with what you have but it works super well and incorporates some of the other methods whilst allowing you to put your own spin on it.

 Walk your environment noting any distinctive points where your horse could target. I allow the horse to take part in this process. We walk together and if there are spots that the horse is comfortable at or the horse stops at then I will take note. For instance my youngster would always opt to go to one particular gateway and take a little breather or look in the field. I also noted that she would sniff a certain bucket on our way to the gateway. Around the corner she liked to stop to munch on a small patch of grass and around the corner from that, there was an apple tree where she would hoover a few up. These were my four points.

Reinforce heavily at each of these four points if the horse stops there. Ask them to target the gates, the bucket or whatever stimuli you are using. Repeat this circuit multiple times so your horse learns the route you are taking and that each point becomes highly reinforcing for them.

 Stand with your horse shoulder to shoulder with your first point in view. I usually have the horse on a long rein or long lead rope during this process because the aim is for them to eventually be walking ahead of you, so you are building their confidence to lead and not be led. Because you have a strong reinforcement history at that point, your horse should naturally start walking towards it to target it. If they don't then you can initiate by taking the first step but gradually allow yourself to fall back. This might take some time, especially if you have a horse that isn't overly confident. I would also suggest reinforcing every step or small try that they take towards to the point.

 Once you have got to your first point and reinforced a few times then you're ready to point your horse in the direction of the next point. For this you will need to use the skills that were taught previously for direction: reinforce every little step and off you go to your next point.

 Once your horse is starting to move to the points then you can add in your chosen VOICE cue. Initially I use "Go touch" or "Go target" because the horse knows the touch or target cue but switch to "Walk on" later.

I have had people question this way of working saying things like "but doesn't the horse get stuck at each point?". This really isn't the case. I find that as the horse grows in confidence they then start to choose to walk past certain points. The points are there to allow the horse to gather itself and take a breather if it needs to, drop thresholds and stand and observe the environment before walking to the next point. A little like a safety blanket. What happens over time is they grow in confidence and then choose to continue moving rather than stop at each point. It's a way of breaking the walk or ride down into incremental steps for the horse so they know they only have to go from the mounting block to point one and then they can calm down and now they know the next point and so on.

IN THE SADDLE

 THINK about moving forward.

 BREATHE in and on your 'out' breath...

 Use your VOICE cue to say "Walk on".

 Use your SEAT by tilting your upper body just slightly forward.

 Here you can present your VISUAL cue if you have a target, but of course if you are using cones then that will already be in place. If you aren't using either then look at your point in the direction you want to go.

 Use your TACTILE cue: your leg. Squeeze with both legs gently and release. Again, we are not escalating the pressure until the horse does as we ask but are just gently squeezing and if your horse doesn't respond then repeat the process from piece one.

The cordeo doesn't need to be fiddled with at all. Just let it hang loose around the horse's neck. If you feel you need it then carry it lightly between your fingers.

BACK UP CUE

Teaching a horse to walk backwards is really simple and there is no need to use any type of force for this exercise.

ON THE GROUND

The easiest way to do this is by starting with the target or luring. I'll share both methods but just be aware that luring can frustrate some horses so as always make sure that you personalise your plan to the character of the horse in front of you.

METHOD ONE

 Stand shoulder to shoulder with your horse or in front of your horse. Some horses find the latter easier in the first instance. THINK about where you'd like your horse to go.

 Present your VISUAL, the target, to your horse but position it so it is just under the chin and ask the horse to target. In order to bop it with their nose they will have to move backwards a little. Click and reinforce as soon as they start to move their feet. Remove target.

At this point it really doesn't matter whether the horse moves a full step backwards, if their back end moves to the left or right or if they don't go fully backwards but sideways instead. We are as always just reinforcing the 'try'. Move on to piece two once the try has been reinforced numerous times.

Present the target a little further back under the chin so the horse has to take one step back. 'Click' the step and reinforce. Once the horse is consistently stepping back then move on.

BREATHE in and on your 'out' breath add in your VOICE cue: "Back up". Repeat numerous times over numerous sessions.

Extend the number of steps you ask for before clicking and reinforcing.

Using the Cordeo for your TACTILE cue lightly bump it a couple of times by taking it lightly between your fingers, bump and release. As before we don't want to increase the pressure but we just ask by bumping and then stop and repeat the process if the horse doesn't respond.

METHOD TWO

Stand shoulder to shoulder with your horse and THINK about how you'd like him to move.

Have some feed in your hand and make a fist.

Present the back of your hand to your horse by its nose. Once the horse realises there is food, slowly bring your hand backwards towards the underside of the horses neck.

When the horse takes a step backwards then 'click' and present your horse with the food in your closed hand.

Once your horse has the hang of what you are doing then add in the VOICE cue "Back up" as you lure him backwards. As soon as he takes the step then, 'Click' and present him with the food.

 Once this has been repeated multiple times and you are confident that your horse understands the behaviour you are asking for then you can phase out your visual cue. You can do this by testing your VOICE cue. Ask for the back up without presenting the food. If your horse doesn't respond, then go back to piece five.

 Add your TACTILE cue by bumping the cordeo once or twice. Click and reinforce as soon as the horse responds.

IN THE SADDLE

 Whilst your horse is at a standstill, THINK about him backing up.

 Lean slightly forward with your SEAT.

 BREATHE in and on your 'out' breath...

 Use your VOICE cue: "Back up".

 Slightly bump your CORDEO once or twice and release.

UPPING THE GAIT

ON THE GROUND

 Set up an inside out round pen or along a fence line. With your horse on the outside and you on the inside start to run. As soon as your horse picks up a trot, 'click' and reinforce. Repeat numerous times.

 Do the same again but this time wait for your horse to take a proper stride, then 'click' and reinforce. Repeat numerous times.

 Do the same again but wait for your horse to take two strides and so on.

 Add in a VOICE cue such as "Trot". Keep repeating over numerous sessions.

 When you feel that your horse understands the voice cue then you can start to phase out your body language. Initially, ask with your voice cue and run with less vigour, then take fewer steps but reinforce your horse for keeping the movement going. Eventually you should just be able to ask with your voice.

IN THE SADDLE

 When your horse has a nice forward walk, THINK trot.

 Use your SEAT by sitting up.

 BREATHE in and on your 'out breath' use your VOICE cue: "trot".

 Use your TACTILE cue by lightly squeezing your legs against your horse's side and releasing. Click and reinforce when your horse responds.

If your horse doesn't respond then you know you need to go backwards a little so he fully understands the voice cue. I'd also recommend taking your horse somewhere where he is that little bit more forward and more likely to offer up a trot. For instance on the way home from a hack. You can also help your horse along by riding out with a buddy and asking the buddy horse to trot and reinforcing when your horse joins in. Be sure to check that this doesn't send him over threshold.

You can repeat this whole process for the canter gait too.

BRIDLELESS RIDING -PROBLEM SOLVING

Generally the problem solving with bridleless riding will be-

-Don't allow your horse to go over threshold. This is paramount with or without a bridle.

-Keep a close eye on body language and stress signals.

-Check your horse can cope in the environment you choose to ride in.

-Go back to the groundwork.

BUT

What happens when things do start to go a little pear shaped?

BREATHE

Remember to stay calm and practise your breathing. As I said before it's amazing how breath control can take a horse from crazy to calm within seconds.

DISMOUNT

If you are worried, then there is absolutely no shame in getting off your horse and walking with him for a while until you feel he

is calmer. Do some simple targeting with him on the ground or any exercises that he knows well and is confident with and this will help him to refocus.

TARGET

Use targeting. By now your horse should be able to generalise so ask him to touch any stimuli that may be around you to help him calm down and come back to you with listening ears and mind.

REINFORCE

If your horse isn't listening well then reinforce the tiny steps. For instance if he wants to go one way but you are asking for another then use your SEAT and TACTILE cues to ask him to go that way. As soon as he turns an ear in the way you want to go, 'click' and reinforce. You've got his attention! Then ask for a head turn in the way you would like to go, 'click' and reinforce. He's a little more tuned in! Ask for a step in the direction that you would like to go and so on!

All of this has to take place before the horse goes over threshold though because once he's gone then there is really no stopping him as flight mode sets in. If that happens then hold on for dear life my love! You're in for a wild ride! HAHA! Joking! If you follow the steps in this book then you should be fine! If your horse goes over threshold, get off and walk with him.

ONE FINAL WORD

So there we have it! Take what you've learnt, put it into practice and have fun in the process! I'd recommend that you keep coming back to these steps and always have your cordeo on your horse so that when you are out and about you can continue to practise with it, even if you don't want to throw the bridle at that particular time.

I would love to hear from you all via my Facebook page 'Beautiful Horsemanship'. Let me know how you are getting on, send me pictures and if you are struggling and need further advice then I'm happy to help! I can't wait to see how you get on!

Printed in Great Britain
by Amazon